BUSINESS PLAN

QuickStart Guide

The Simplified Beginner's Guide to Writing A Business Plan

contents

BEFORE YOU START READING, DOWNLOAD YOUR FREE DIGITAL ASSETS!

Visit the URL below to access your free Digital Asset files that are included with the purchase of this book.

☑ Summaries
☑ Cheat Sheets
☑ Articles

☑ White Papers
☑ Charts & Graphs
☑ Reference Materials

DOWNLOAD YOURS HERE:

www.clydebankmedia.com/businessplan-assets

introduction

Bravo to you for having the initiative, drive, vision and passion to create your own business! It can be a scary proposition and certainly a riskier one when compared to working for someone else your entire life, but it's an endeavor that usually pays off if you approach the development phase correctly and continue your dedication to the business by honing good habits and management skills.

The process of getting started can be daunting for many people, and it is common for individuals to fall into a "paralysis by analysis" situation, failing to take the necessary actions to start their businesses simply because they don't know how or because they are overwhelmed by the details. To those who are unfamiliar with the world of starting a business, the multitude of steps, complexity of commitments, and technicalities associated with successful commerce can be staggering. This book will shed light on this process and will teach you how to write a business plan that can turn a great idea into an amazing business.

We'll start with the fundamentals, explaining exactly why you need a business plan, when you should create it, and what information you'll need before you start writing. From there, we will dive deeper into the specific chapters, or sections, of your plan and teach you the shortcuts that will allow you to generate this content quickly without sacrificing quality.

So, follow us into the world of entrepreneurship as we slowly unravel the steps to a solid business plan.

1

Why, When, & How

Let's start with the basics:

What is a Business Plan?

While you might have a great idea for a business of your own, chances are there are simply too many factors to keep track of in your head. That's why it's important to write them down and, hence, to formalize your business goals and methods for building the business. This will orient you as you develop the first stages of your business and will allow you to convey your plan to others plainly and simply. The need to clearly share your plan with others very important because, even if you are a sole proprietor (single-person business owner), you may still need to talk to banks, financial advisors, lawyers, or potential investors about your business. A well-written and comprehensive business plan will give them the information they need and inspire them to trust you and, hopefully, invest in you as well.

Who Needs a Business Plan?

This is a trick question because everyone needs a business plan, no matter which field or industry you wish to enter. A new startup company needs a business plan. An established business that's looking to expand needs a business plan. If you are in the world of business and strive to be successful, a business plan is always essential.

> *"There are so many options when it comes to starting a business, including the size, location, and, of course, the reason for existence,"* note the experts at Entrepreneur Magazine in their book entitled Write Your Business Plan. *"You'll be able to determine all of these and so many more aspects of business with the help of your business plan. It forces you to think through all of the areas that form the main concept to the smallest details. This way, you don't find yourself remembering at the last minute that your website still isn't developed or that you still have most of your inventory in a warehouse and no way to ship it."*

You will find that, as a business owner, the business plan that you create in the beginning is helpful throughout the extent of your organization's operations. Your plan will grow and develop as your company grows and develops. Remember that a business plan lays out goals and the methods for achieving them; you will continually modify your business plan as your company realizes its goals and as priorities change.

Why Write a Business Plan?

First and foremost, research has shown that prospective business owners are two-and-a-half times more likely to actually go into business if they take the time to write a business plan. With only that statistic in mind, you can easily discern that writing a plan is time well spent if you're serious about reaching your entrepreneurial goals. Why is this statistic true? Those who take the time to write business plans have proven that they are willing to take the extra steps necessary to get their business off to a good start.

Business plans are used for a variety of reasons, but one of their main purposes is to show potential investors your business' overall goals and strategies. Investors like to see all of your research in one neat and tidy document. They like knowing that you've done ample research and have the ability to follow through with that research. Many business owners will tell you that writing a business plan was an essential step during the initial stages of business development because it helped to organize their thoughts before meeting with investors and making major business decisions.

A well-written business plan acts as a template to guide decisions and conceptualization through a checklist of important items. When addressing these items mentally it can be easy to overlook developmental concerns such as marketing strategy and operational finances, start-up costs, business management, and organization. Thinking through all of these individual details during the development and conceptualization phase of your plan will take the larger concepts and focus them into specific areas of interest.

Writing a business plan is a proven positive guide for getting your business off the ground and taking it from the drawing board to the boardroom. It's even required by many investors.

When Should I Write My Business Plan?

Every time you think about your potential business and jot down details you wish to recall at a later time, you're contributing to your eventual business plan. As a matter of fact, you may already have much of it written though it's not yet in "plan" form.

Now, as you get ready to do things such as look for partners or investors, find a location (if needed), choose a business entity, and hire managers or employees, it's time to collect all those notes and formalize your plan.

Tim Berry of Entrepreneur describes a business plan as a work in progress and notes that, even though you may need to show it to others eventually, it is first for YOU and no one else.

> *"Do it because it helps you divide and manage big goals into practical steps,"* he explains. *"Instead of looking at it as a document, think of your business plan as a place on your computer where you collect ideas, useful stories, lists and numbers. It's a place where you keep track of the market, your milestones, goals and projections."*

That said, if you're seeking a less ethereal answer as to when to put your collection into a well-written document, experts say that you should do it when you're ready to take those ideas and make them real; when you're willing to invest money and time in all those things you wrote down on the tablet by your bed or in the "notes" section of your iPhone. It's that simple.

You can also use your business plan to watch how your business progresses throughout the first weeks, months and years. This establishment of goals acts as a baseline to which you will compare your actual results. If you project that your company will have certain profits by the end of a quarter or that you will have so many employees, you can check those things against your business plan. This demonstrates the dynamic nature of business goals and statements of goals. As goals are met and new challenges appear, business owners, managers, and decision makers must be both proactive and responsive to changing conditions.

How Long Should My Business Plan Be?

Overall, business plans should be direct and concise. They should be straightforward, well-organized, and not convoluted. You will find that it's easier to present a well-written business plan to investors and others, and as an organizational tool it will be easier to revisit if it's well-written.

A few tips to making your business plan as effective as possible :

Consider using shorter sentences.

Long sentences don't necessarily impress. Generally, anyone other than you who might be reading your plan probably won't read every word. They'll skim. Skimming is easier with short, concise sentences. If your sentences are too long or complicated, the reader might miss key concepts.

Avoid using acronyms or technical jargon.

If you feel that you need these terms in your plan, explain them briefly. You can't always assume that your readers know what you know. If you're presenting the plan face-to-face, offer to respond to questions at the end of the presentation of your business plan to clear up any ambiguities, or periodically break up your presentation with opportunities for questions. For technically-complex topics, consider including a glossary of terms at the end of each section, if you deem it necessary.

Use bullet points for lists.

Visual organization of information will help your readers stay focused and help to emphasize the most important items for review. Well-defined sections, a comprehensive index, and other organizational tools will help your reader easily search throughout the document to find information again and again as needed. If your business plan is conveyed digitally, consider using hyperlinks throughout the document to connect concepts or allow readers to jump to definitions of terms.

When using bulleted lists, avoid compiling a bare list.

Using sub-bullets or explanatory paragraphs below will answer questions before they are asked and will send the message that you have considered every detail. This is especially important when conveying goals, strategies, or product features.

Keep it short.

Today's average business plan is approximately forty pages long. You will need approximately 20-30 pages of regular text for all the necessary sections of the business plan and then about ten pages of appendices. More about that will be addressed later, but it's important to note that if your business plan extends to more than 40 pages long, it's worth another review as there is probably extraneous material that can be eliminated.

Graphics are the exception.

When you add lots of graphics to your business plan, it can add length, of course. If this happens, don't fret. You can still use the forty-page rule; just see how it measures without the graphics. Graphics can include pictures of your product(s), possible locations, menus, floor plans, and logos. All of these can be very useful and readers often find them interesting.

Charts can do the same thing.

Consider bar graphs or pie charts that enhance the content. Flowcharts, maps of workflow, and any other relevant visual aids should be used. The phrase "a picture is worth a thousand words" has never been more applicable. Using neat and well-formed graphics will inform your audience quickly and effectively and will increase the ease with which your plan is shared.

Choose your font wisely.

Perhaps this goes without saying, but use a very readable font that is a normal standard. You can change the font for your headings or for graphics, but a best practice is to stick to only two different fonts for your entire document. Keep it simple; keep it readable.

Use spellcheck!

Perhaps this also goes without saying as well, but be sure to double-check spelling and proofread before you print your final draft. If grammar and punctuation aren't your strong point, have a friend or colleague review your plan. Make sure to double-check your numbers, too. This is something that an outside proofreader can't check; it's your responsibility! You wouldn't want to be embarrassed when your figures don't add up. A small oversight can have disastrous ramifications for your presentation and, therefore, your loan.

Hopefully, we've addressed some of your initial questions and concerns about business plans. It's important that you feel confident about writing your business plan before you get started. Make sure you are organized as you go into the construction portion of your plan; build an outline and stick to it.

| 2 |

Do Your Homework

Before you (finally) get started writing your own business plan, there's some homework to do. This is the part of the construction process in which you tackle research and exploration. Once you have collected all pertinent information, you can begin to outline your goals and objectives.

Here are some important points to research :

Research Your Potential Markets

Start to think about and analyze who is actually going to use the products and/or services that you will be offering. This shouldn't be a "guesstimation". You should actually hit the proverbial pavement and conduct real interviews, collect data, and ask questions of people to whom you will be selling.

One of the most important questions you must ask yourself when you begin to formulate your business ideas is whether or not there is a market for your product or service in your area. Hopefully, the answer to this question is "yes". If you truly believe there may not be a market for your product in your area, but you're still passionate about opening your business, you might need to consider relocating. But first, take some time to think outside the box, because usually with a little creativity there is a market for just about anything. It just needs to be presented in the right way and you might need to market your products or service differently. Alternately, if you were set on opening a bricks-and-mortar location but think that perhaps it won't succeed, you could opt to change your business model to an e-commerce-based design.

This provides the flexibility to sell from anywhere to everywhere and does not limit you geographically. Of course, however, not every model can be brought online.

After you have determined that there is in fact a market for your product or service, further follow-up questions will be necessary. Seek answers about local demographics including age groups, gender, ethnicities, and economic populations. Compile this data so you can easily access it later when you write your business plan or whenever the need arises. If researching your target demographic becomes a brick wall for you, consider one of a number of market research services available to future business owners. For a pre-determined price, these companies will conduct market research on your behalf. These organizations are experts in market data collection and have the resources to identify the distribution of local demographics quickly and accurately. If their price tag is within your budget, their information can be a tremendous asset and may make the difference between a green light on a business plan or the red light that nips a prospect in the bud. It is better to know before implementation that a project will fail than to see it through to the end with nothing to show.

Market research companies aren't cheap. However, a wealth of free resources exists that can help you compile similar statistics. Census data, public records, chamber of commerce studies, and independent studies exist at little or no cost to those seeking information. Combining public or easily-obtainable information with interviews, questionnaires, and other information-gathering techniques can answer your questions (and, therefore, the questions your investors may have) and provide a foundation for your research.

Regardless of your choice in market research methods, this is one of the most important pieces of research to tackle. You will learn invaluable information that will guide you through the rest of the business planning process, and the data gathered here can shape the entire direction of your business.

Determine Potential Market Size

Everyone has big dreams of becoming extremely successful. Those dreams aren't impossible, but in reality you may need to start small. As a strong foundation is built, the scaling of operations becomes possible. As the saying goes, "Rome wasn't built in a day."

Along with analyzing your market, you need to consider your market size and number of potential customers. Information regarding that market's spending habits, average levels of disposable income, age, employment, and ethnicity makeup is also critically important, as we mentioned previously. Different groups of people will behave in different ways; this is science and anthropology at its simplest. Understanding and predicting those behaviors allows decision makers to effectively plan their business.

You might start out thinking that you have hundreds of thousands of potential customers, but that scale could be out of your reach at the beginning. Think of it this way: you've invented a new line of toothpaste – a product that everyone uses, right? So potentially, your market size could be the entire population of the world. That seems crazy and unthinkable now, but consider popular toothpaste brands that really do market to the entire world. They had to start somewhere, right? It is possible to get there, but you need to start with a smaller market size and work your way up to larger markets.

Start with toothpaste that specifically targets one group of people, like children or people with dentures. After you've narrowed your market, you can start to ask yourself more specific questions about that market group:

- How many children need toothpaste in any given community?
- How many people with dentures currently live in the United States?

- How much toothpaste do people use in a month or a year?
- Is there a substitute product, or a product that people could use instead of toothpaste?
- Who else are you competing against in the toothpaste market?
- What benefits do consumers perceive about your competitor's offerings & how do you compete with these features?

Note : The word 'perceive' is used here because consumer perception is based on a multitude of factors including but not limited to experience, advertising, preference, and brand loyalty. It is important to understand that there is no difference between customer perception and their interpretation of the reality of your brand. You may have heard the phrase "perception is everything," but a better statement, at least relating to consumers, is "perception is reality." This underscores the importance of thorough market research and the power of marketing and advertising.

By asking yourself these questions and similar questions, you can begin to learn where you fit into your market.

Understanding Competition

Competition between different members of the same industry or market is not always as simple as which company can produce the lowest cost goods. Think back to your own experience. There must have been a time when you were willing to spend more money in the name of quality. When you purchased your cellphone, price may not have been the only factor. Features such as speed, memory size, and ease of use may have enticed you to pay for a model that was not the cheapest. This is indicative of a market with high product differentiation, a market in which a product or service is assessed for more than just price. This is considered a value-impacted market

Now think of the purchase of a product like coal or iron. These are considered commodities, or products that have little differentiation between sources and for which price is the distinguishing characteristic. It is important to understand where your product falls in relation to both ends of this spectrum because products that are commoditized, or largely the same but differentiated by cost, require a totally different manner of thinking than products that are value-driven, or take into account features other than price.

Into which quadrant does the product or service you are selling fall? The answer is a mix of your informed opinion and the reactions of the people that you interview and poll. How do you compete? The answer is with competitive edge. What sets your product apart from others on the market? Is your toothpaste simply cheaper, or does it offer superior plaque and sensitivity protection?

Competitive edge can manifest itself in a number of ways. You may have developed a faster, cheaper, and more efficient method of producing toothpaste. That means competing with price is an option. You may have developed a method of creating toothpaste that makes visits to the dentist obsolete. That's competing based on value. If that process is cheaper than the market standard, you're in the most desirable quadrant: the upper right or competition based on cost and value.

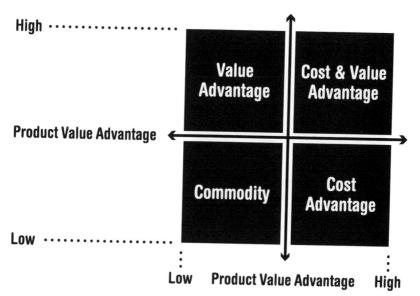

 fig. 1 : The Commodity Matrix. Products that have no value advantage and compete solely on price occupy the lower left quadrant. These are products like coal and iron. Products that occupy other quadrants have a mix of value and cost advantage.

What Do You Need to Get Started?

Sit down and make a list of things you need to get yourself up and running as a company. Some of the things you will need are simple and easy to obtain, like office supplies and computers, while others are much more complicated, like employees and product designs. You'll obviously need plenty of tangible things for your business to get off the ground, but there are plenty of intangible things, too, like market research and potential customers (in the form of prospects and leads), to make it all come together. At this point, don't be afraid to make the list as detailed as possible

This is the time for you to think through every step you need to take before your company launches, and all the things that could stand in the way of that happening. It is important at this stage to be thorough, but new challenges will arise, goals will be met, and new goals will replace those original ones. Focus on the process from where you are to where you want to be, but don't get frazzled if new information crops up. Roll with the punches and incorporate the new information into your business plan as you go.

Make Product Samples

Potential investors want to see the product or products in which they are investing, so you'll need to have product samples to show off when you pitch your business plan. If you are offering a service instead of a product, be prepared to demonstrate your service either in person or via a video demonstration. If you are opening a restaurant, invite potential investors for a meal and serve them a few dishes that will be on the menu. There are ample ways to show investors your products and services even if it is something they can't hold in their hands. This is an opportunity for you to express your creativity and make a lasting impression on the people who ultimately may end up bankrolling your business.

In addition, future employees will also be interested in seeing product samples and testing your services. You will need to show them that your company is worth their time and effort. They'll want to know that your company is going to be successful and they aren't going to be looking for work in six months' time. Potential employees should also be excited about your products and services so that they can sell with passion and sincerity. That kind of dedication and excitement is contagious, and if your employees are sold on your brand's product and vision, that will translate into sales for you.

Initially your product samples may be homemade, and although that may work just fine, you still want a product sample that says "wow" when you pull it out of the box. Take your initial model and dress it up a little to impress your audience. This may cost a bit more, but if the difference between a "bleh" and a "wow" presentation means spending a few extra dollars, the money is well spent.

Find Possible Locations to Rent/Buy

It's time to go location hunting. Although you may not actually be renting out a space for a few months or more, you'll need to research the type of space you need. The only way you'll be able to do that is by actually seeing what is available and how much the space costs.

Contact a real estate broker and have him or her walk you through several available retail spaces in neighborhoods in which you are interested in locating your business. You will have targeted these areas because you have already done your market research. Keep accurate records of all the places you see so you can compare the cost, square footage, and other important details later.

You will quickly learn what you can get for your money in each of your chosen neighborhoods and can determine how that will affect your decisions.

Note : Rarely do novice business owners buy a location for their business, but it can happen if you find a steal of a deal or the perfect location. If you are interested in buying a location for your business, you can speak to your real estate broker about this as well. You will need to factor that into your start-up costs and that large expense will later need to be recovered through sales.

Determine Start-up Costs

Start-up costs can be startling but it's essential to know exactly what your initial outlay will be. Sit down and make a list of everything you need to get your business going. This is different from the list you made earlier, because this list includes only the things that cost money. It doesn't include the market research and potential customers, though it is important to be mindful of hidden costs associated with those activities. Everything from cash registers to industrial kitchen equipment and tables will need to be factored into the start-up costs.

You'll need to think about aesthetics too, such as the cost of painting the walls and adding appropriate light fixtures to your new location. Try to be reasonable and conservative with your spending. There will be time and money to renovate or upgrade later.

Cover the basics or the most important things first, and then, down the road when you are turning a good profit, you can consider adding a few of the more expensive extras. Do some research to find where you can take advantage of the best prices for the items you need. There are plenty of places online that offer discounts for ordering in bulk, and comparison shopping can be a fantastic asset now and in the future. Since you will probably be ordering things in larger quantities, see if you can find these types of websites or stores. Also build relationships with other local businesses that might offer your discounts if you buy their products in bulk. In addition, there are numerous B2B (business to business) organizations that specialize in providing new businesses with the total package they need to get their business off the ground.

Here are a few things to remember when factoring in your start-up costs (there could be more, depending on your business):

- Rent
- Utilities
- Salaries
- Equipment

- Maintenance for Equipment
- Supplies
- Legal Licenses or Permits
- Marketing & Promotion

Speaking with a lawyer that specializes in business law and/or perhaps a business accountant is wise, in many cases. Business lawyers, though charging by the minute, can be a valuable resource and can work with you to develop a checklist to ensure you don't make any costly errors in the future.

Basic business accounting can be more or less straightforward, but experts agree that hiring an accountant is often the safest (though not the cheapest) route. Other options, like QuickBooks or do-it-yourself business accounting programs, exist for your use as well.

Potential investors will want to see that you have compiled a thoughtful and thorough list of your start-up costs, down to the very last paperclip. Make an organized chart that breaks out each part of your costs so your investors can see how the money will be allocated rather than simply noting that you'll need $100,000 to get started, for example. An investor wants to know that the amount you've stated is indeed appropriate, which can be demonstrated when each cost is itemized and each dollar is justified.

If you are struggling as to how to estimate your start-up costs, there is a free online calculator that helps to break down your costs for the first six months. It assists in calculating and showing your potential revenue as well. To find the online calculator, click Online Start-Up Costs Calculator.

Who are Your Potential Investors?

You might have the best business idea in the world, but unless you're prepared to foot the bill in total, without the backing of a bank or investor(s), you aren't going to reach a single customer. People don't lend money just because they like you (though that's certainly a plus!) or even because you have a good idea. There are specific guidelines that you must meet in order for them to invest in your dream. Obviously, if your idea is a good one, then you've taken the first positive step, but you'll have to take it just a little further in order to secure a loan and make your dream of owning a business a reality.

Banks and other lenders generally look at a potential business' capital, capacity, collateral, conditions, and character (the "5C's of lending"), to determine whether or not they will invest. Let's discuss what each of these 5C's means to you, so you can prepare yourself and make sure you are prepared when you talk with potential investors about your business.

Capital

This refers to your sources of income other than the business you are trying to open. The bank wants to know that if you lose your job or the business goes under, there are other means to repay the loan, such as investments, savings, or assets.

Capacity

The bank will want to know how you handle debt and whether you can manage this new debt with your current income. They will judge this debt against any current debt you may already have. This is called a debt-to-income ratio. Any former employment and previous debt may also come into play.

As your business develops, investors will also want to know the planned liquidity of your business. Liquidity is the ability to pay off short-term debt obligations. It can be measured by a number of liquidity ratios, the most common being the current ratio. The current ratio measures current assets against current liabilities (debts) and its formula is expressed as follows: Acceptable current ratios vary from industry to industry, but many industries consider a value of between 1 and 3 to be acceptable. A value of 1 would mean that for every dollar your business has in assets, it would have a dollar in liabilities. A business with positive cash flow and a current ratio of 1 will have no problem repaying short-term debts as they become due.

Investors understand that emerging businesses will have significantly more liabilities, both short-term and long-term, but presenting them with a plan to bring your business up to a higher level of liquidity will provide them with a higher level of assurance that your business can repay its short-term debt.

Note : It is worth noting that a company with too high of a liquidity ratio is also a risk for investors. Companies with too high a current ratio value may be misusing their assets and wasting working capital through poor management.

Collateral

This only applies if you are requesting a secured loan. A secured loan means that you are placing something as collateral against the loan. Think of an auto loan or a home equity loan. When you assume those loans, there is a car or house that the bank holds as collateral against the value of the loan. If the loan isn't repaid, the bank can attempt to salvage the loss with the value of the collateral; i.e. they'll repossess your car or foreclose on your house. If you apply for a secured loan, you are offering something as collateral against either a partial value of the loan or the loan's entire value.

Conditions

The bank can ask how you plan to use the money they are loaning to you. This can be very general or very specific, so you may need to be prepared to account for every dollar you are requesting. If you plan to purchase a vehicle for your business, they may want to know, and they may want to inspect the vehicle in order to approve the loan. A loan officer may be assigned to you and may place very specific conditions on your loan that you must follow in order for the loan to be approved.

Character

This is also sometimes referred to as credit history instead of character, because the bank will pull your credit report and review it will a fine tooth comb. They will want to know every detail of your credit history, and approval of your loan will be based on that content.

Have you defaulted on a loan? If so, be prepared to defend yourself, because your track record looks sketchy. Luckily, credit history does improve with time, and if you defaulted years ago, it may not be evident now. Generally, negative credit history entries are removed from an individual's report after seven years with the exception of bankruptcies, which have a reporting lifespan of ten years.

If you are interested in seeing your credit score before you go to the bank, you can check it for free in a number of ways. However, there are many imposter websites online, so be wary of giving out your personal information to phishing scams or other phony services. The three credit reporting agencies - TransUnion, Equifax and Experian - are required by law to provide you with a free credit report once every twelve months. If you are interested in seeing your credit scores, you can visit: _www.annualcreditreport.com_

Finding your potential investors and making sure that you are prepared with all the information you need to win them over is the key to securing financing. Now that you've done your research and you're prepared with all the right strategies, you are ready to start writing your actual business plan.

| 3 |

Summary & Company Description

The typical business plan has eight different parts, plus a possible ninth part - the appendix - for all the extra things that don't fit anywhere else. We will explain each part of the business plan in detail.

Part 1 : Executive Summary

Many people suggest leaving this piece until you've finished everything else. It is arguably the most important part of your business plan, because it is the first thing anyone examining your plan will read and will be the way that those reading about your business can get to know you. If you are just getting your thoughts organized, this isn't where you want to start. Start with parts 2-8, and then come back to this when you feel more prepared to write this in an organized, professional manner. At the very least, if you choose to start here, revisit this piece at least once, if not more, after you've finished your entire business plan to make sure your initial draft hasn't strayed from any changes made in later sections.

Note : This list is for both established businesses and start-ups. If you are a start-up, you won't have as much information to include as an established business will have, or your information may be slightly different. Feel free to modify the information as necessary to fit your needs.

What to include in your Executive Summary:

Mission Statement

Take your time with this. It should be at least several sentences or a short paragraph, and it should clearly describe your business objectives. Jack Welch, the transformational former CEO of General Electric and business guru, says that an effective mission statement answers the question "How are we going to win in this business?" He believes, after years of experience, that this is the most effective way to convey your business' mission to the world, and that winning should be your business objective. Winning can mean that you've accomplished all your goals and you went home tired and fulfilled. Winning can mean changing lives. Simply put, you know why you want to start (or have started) this business, and your mission statement encapsulates and spreads that passion to those who interact with you professionally. This statement sets the tone for the rest of your business plan presentation and the business relationships you will cultivate in the future years to come.

Company Information

Include all the information you can about your business name, the founders, the number of employees, and location(s). Established businesses will obviously have more information in this section. Include any details you consider pertinent.

Company Growth

Talk about how the company has grown since it first started, including profits, employees, and market share. New businesses can skip this section.

Products/Services

Use a few sentences to talk about the products and/or services you will offer to customers. If you are an established business, talk about what you already offer and what you plan to offer in the future, if you are expanding. Use concrete terms and define your offerings or service plan with confident words and phrases.

Financial Information

If you are an established business, you'll need to include your current financial information (i.e., your bank or investors). It doesn't need to be too detailed; general information is fine. Again, new businesses do not need to include this section.

Brief Summary of Future Plans

Talk about your goals for the business. Where do you see the business at the end of one year, five years, ten years? Planning at the ten-year mark will be understandably vague. Try to think about where you want to take the business you are starting and draw upon the trends you uncovered through due diligence. Investors and future partners will want you to demonstrate long-term planning and goal setting skills.

Start-ups don't have a lot of this information, so just focus on the information you do have. You can include details about your market analysis and why you believe your business will be successful in the area you've chosen. You can talk about how you feel your product or service will fill a need in the community or in your particular target market. That will lead perfectly into the summary of your future plans.

The executive summary should only be a single page, which means every word you put on that page needs to be chosen carefully. Your executive summary needs to grab your readers and pull them into your business, making them excited to learn more about what you are planning. You need to show how your business is going to be successful and sell every aspect of not only your business but yourself as well. It is important to bring your reader on board with your passion.

Part 2 : Company Description

This is the section in which you actually pitch your business to your readers. In the previous section, you attracted their interest and enticed them to learn more about your business.

Focus on these specific items in your company description:

Goals

Talk about your specific goals for the company. You'll want to express your vision for the company and how you plan to make that vision a reality. Do this in a fairly succinct way without too many specific details.

What You're All About

Explain what makes your business unique and different from everyone else. If you're opening a smoothie shop, what makes your smoothie shop stand out from the hundreds of smoothie shops that already exist? Why should an investor look at your shop differently than the others? Give them a reason to love yours above the rest.

Marketplace Needs

This is where you discuss a hole you have found in the market that you believe needs to be filled. There will be an entire section of your business plan dedicated to talking about your market, so only briefly mention this here.

How Your Products or Services Meet the Needs

After talking about how the marketplace has needs to be filled, you will move into discussing how your products or services will fill that gap. Look back at your description of how your business is unique, how it produces competitive edge, and then match this with the need in the marketplace. As these two characteristics fuse together, you establish how your business will be successful.

Who You Serve

Next, you'll want your readers to understand exactly to whom you are trying to sell your products or services. Take the time to talk about your target customer. You've done your research, and you've already made this determination. You already know if you're targeting stay at home moms, children, or retired veterans, for example, so provide that information in this section.

How Will You Be Successful?

As you continue moving forward, you will need a few advantages over your competition, and your readers need to see them. What do you have up your sleeve?

Don't be afraid to outline what gives you a competitive edge or your core competencies in specific terms. Competitive edge is a combination of different business elements that blend together to put your company above competitors. In the instance of a smoothie shop, competitive edge could be better-tasting smoothies, quick service, or a prime location. Core competencies are attributes that you have mastered and are leveraging to produce competitive edge. To produce better-tasting smoothies, you could have access to unique recipes, for example. Quicker service, perhaps, could be the product of industry-new equipment not available to other shops in the area.

Any of these could be listed as advantages:

- Key Location
- Expert Employees
- Efficient Operations
- Ability to Operate Cheaper (always include an explanation)

Your company description does not need to be long. Keep it short and concise, and try not to overdo anything as you explain operations. It is often best to keep the company description to more than a page but less than two pages long.

Your company description is almost as important as the executive summary, because this is where you really get to pitch your goals and the uniqueness of your ideas. It's your chance to show others why they should fall in love with your company as much as you have and how your core competencies will back up your operations.

| 4 |

Market Analysis & Organization

Let's look at the next two parts of your business plan. In the first section, we are going to look at the market analysis and get into deeper explanations of the market results you found while researching. The second part explains the structure and organization of your business.

Part 3 : Market Analysis

The market analysis will be one of the largest sections of your business plan. There's much information to present and include, both generally and specifically, in regards to your business.

Below is a list of the information that you should include in your market analysis:

Industry Description & Future

This is a very general description of the industry you are joining. Talk about the industry's current size and what kind of growth it has seen in the past few years, as well as the expected rate of growth over the next few years. If there are any other interesting trends about your industry that you think are relevant or helpful to include here, you should do so. It's also important to include any major customer groups that exist inside your industry.

Your Target Market

After discussing the industry as a whole, define the piece of the industry that you plan to target. We stated earlier that you usually can't target everyone at the start. It's time to narrow your focus and define your target market. As you define your target, there are certain characteristics of your market that are important to mention. They are discussed below.

Classifying Characteristics

Every target market has characteristics that separate it from everyone else, including factors such as age, gender, ethnicity, or job. Which is it? After you've defined its unique characteristics, look at its needs. Are they being met? Do they have a need that your product or service can fill? Is there anything about this group of people that will affect your sales?

Size of Your Target Market

Now that you've decided on a target market, you can find its approximate size. It will take a little research, but you should be able to determine approximately how many people exist in your target market. A variety of marketing solutions software and studies exist to aid in your research, in addition to publically available resources. You will also need to project whether your target market is going to grow, decline or stay the same in the next 10 years.

Market Share

Find out how much of the market is available to you. You obviously can only make an educated guess at this, but be prepared to back up your calculations with real logic indicating how you arrived at your numbers. To calculate market share, use simple division. You calculate the number of projected sales for a specific product or service. Then divide that number by the number of sales the industry has done as a whole for that particular product or service. Multiply that figure by 100, and you get market share.

fig. 2

U.S. Share of Searches
(March 2008)

Google: 69.4%
Yahoo: 14.8%
Bing: 10.2%
Ask: 3.7%
Others: .6%

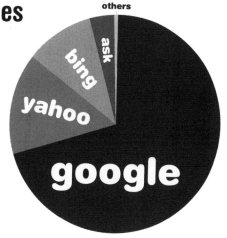

The graph above shows a breakdown for all the web searches done online in 2008. You can see how the market share is divided between the different companies. Obviously Google and Yahoo have the greatest market share. Most small companies do just fine with a market share of two or three percent, so don't feel discouraged if your projected market share is small.

Conduct a market analysis and see where your company fits in the current market and industry. From where are your customers coming? Is there room for you in the mix?

Pricing Structure & Gross Margin Targets

In this section, explain how you plan to price your products and services. Every product and/or service you offer should have a price, but there should also be an explanation for that price. This doesn't need to be overly complicated, but it does need to be researched and well thought out. Price is a key component of what those in the industry call the marketing mix. The marketing mix, or the four P's of marketing, outlines four characteristics that determine how attractive a product will be to consumers.

fig. 3

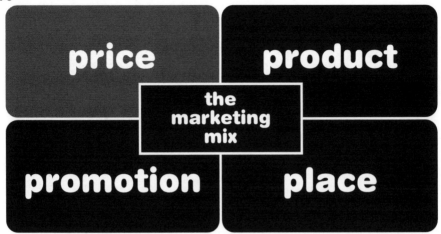

Price refers to the asking price your customers will see when your product hits the shelves. The sticker price should cover the cost to produce the product plus other business expenses, and will need to leave room for profit at the end. Understanding how much to charge your customers comes from understanding how much your product costs to produce and how much your business costs to operate. To determine how many units must be sold to break even, or to recover the cost of production, it becomes necessary to calculate a break-even point. Let's take a look at how to do that.

$$\text{Total Cost} = F + VcQ$$

Where F is your fixed cost, Vc is the variable cost per unit, and Q is the quantity or number of units sold.

Fixed costs are costs that do not fluctuate regardless of the number of products produced. Examples include manufacturing overhead, insurance, and taxes. Variable cost does fluctuate and is dependent on the quantity of products produced. Variable costs could be direct materials, components, and labor.

$$\text{Revenue} = SpQ$$

Where Sp is the selling price and Q is the quantity of products sold.

A break-even point is the recovery of your costs, so the point at which the value for total cost equals the value for revenue tells you the minimum number of units you must sell to break even. Any sales past that point will contribute to profit. This produces the following equation:

$$\text{Total Cost} = \text{Revenue}$$
$$F + VcQ = SpQ$$

Solving for Q at the break-even point (Qbe) produces the following equation:

$$Qbe = \frac{F}{Sp\text{-}Vc}$$

Let's calculate an example. For your proposed business, Superfruit Smoothies, you have determined that your fixed costs per period will be $6,290. Based on the ingredients and your recipes, you also know that the variable cost per unit will be $1.46. To maintain a competitive price, you have determined that you cannot sell your smoothies for more than $5.99 per unit. Feeding that information into the formula, you get the following:

F = $6,290	Qbe = 6,290 / (5.99-1.46)
Vc = $1.46	Qbe = 6,290 / 4.53
Sp = $5.99	Qbe = 1,389 (rounded)

So to recoup your money during this period, you would need to sell nearly 1,400 smoothies at $5.99 each. This is a very helpful formula for modeling your selling price because you can experiment with different prices to see how changes would affect your business. You can calculate that same formula with a selling price of $5.49, or see how adding more expensive ingredients would affect the number you must sell in order to recoup your costs. What if the recipe was changed, lowering the variable cost? What if you negotiate a lower rent, lowering your fixed cost? What if the city levies a new tax on establishments that serve food, thus raising your fixed cost? All of these scenarios can be modeled through the application of the break-even formula.

Knowing your break-even point unlocks many different metrics about your business. Let's say that the period you measured was a year. You have a small smoothie stand that you operate out of your house with your family as the employees. If your fixed costs are spread out evenly over that one-year period, then you can determine how many smoothies you have to sell in a month, a week, or a day. If you need 1,389 smoothies in a year, then you need to sell at least 116 a month (rounded), 29 a week, and approximately five a day (you're closed Sundays). If you are a busy commercial smoothie shop, that fixed cost figure could be the expenses for a single month, or even a week meaning you would have to adjust your later calculations accordingly. When calculating your break-even point it is recommended that you use larger fixed cost periods to produce an accurate representation of your cost profile. The fixed costs for a fiscal year or quarter are both good recommendations.

Start your calculations with what you think your market is willing to pay for the product. This can be based on your own opinion, and it might be too high and it might be too low. You can raise and lower your price as you go, but you have to start somewhere, so choose a number.

Then see what your competitors are charging for the same or similar products and services. How does it compare to what you are charging? Are you overpriced, underpriced or just about right? Choose your price based on the amount of products or services you plan to sell. This will ultimately determine your profit margins. If you are too low with your price and sell a moderate amount, you won't turn a very high profit. Same goes for if you are too high and sell a few, it's all about finding a good balance.

Another consideration for your pricing structure is whether or not you are going to offer sales, bonuses, or rewards to customers. This is a very popular strategy for businesses today and definitely something worth considering. You can establish loyalty programs or reward systems with points or gift cards. The options are truly endless, but customers enjoy being treated well, and they will go where they feel special.

When you project your gross margin target, you are looking into the future and making an educated guess about where your company is going to be in six months, a year, two years, five years and ten years. These should be realistic and informed guesses. You know, perhaps, that at first you will struggle and probably won't turn as much of an initial profit, if any. The most important thing is to be realistic and yet optimistic when determining your gross margin target.

Note : When you reference your research during this section, don't get too detailed. You can mention the results you found, but then you should refer your reader to the appendix, where he or she can see more detailed information about the source. This section is designed for you to provide the results rather than details of your research.

Analyze Your Competition

The final item that needs to be included in your market analysis in an overview of your competition. You should give a quick but detailed analysis of any and all companies against whom you are competing for customers. All of these questions and statements fall under the heading of a SWOT analysis. SWOT stands for Strengths, Weaknesses, Opportunities, and Threats. Keep these four concepts in mind when assessing your competition, your business, and any future detailed decisions.

- Their Current Market Share
- Strengths & Weaknesses (yours and theirs)

fig. 4

As you analyze your competition, you may realize that there are a few other potential obstacles you may encounter. Consider them and take some time to write down how you might deal with them. These might include:

- Is there a seasonal market that you would like to avoid or utilize?
- Does your market have secondary or indirect competitors that could impact you?

- Are there other obstacles in this market (changing technology, no qualified personnel)?

Once you have finished your pricing strategy, you have completed your market analysis. As mentioned, this section will probably be the longest section in your business plan. Don't worry too much about the length as long as you have included everything and kept your wording concise and to the point.

Part 4 : Organization & Management

In this section, you lay out how your business is going to be run, managed and organized. It will include details about ownership of the company and basic profiles for the most important people in the company, as well as the qualifications for board members (or equivalent). You may not have all of these people on staff yet, but your readers want to know as much information as possible. If the same person does multiple jobs in your company, that's okay. Just make it apparent in the business plan and include the qualifications for that person so that your reader knows why that person has the ability to do multiple jobs.

Salary and benefits for your employees should be included in this section. If you are offering any incentives for your employees, they should be listed also, as well as any promotions or options. Help your reader know that these people aren't just names on a piece of paper; they are real people who are also invested in this company.

You should include in your organization and management section a chart that helps to illustrate how the company is organized. You can easily create something similar to the illustration above, replacing the silhouettes with names, or you may provide a simple organizational chart to help readers understand how your company is organized. To further increase the personable and relatable element of your presentation, include headshots of each staff member in addition to their names and qualifications.

Your company's ownership should be clearly explained in this section as well. You'll need to reveal whether you've decided to be a sole proprietor or a general or limited partnership. Or, if you've incorporated your business, identify whether it is a C or S corporation. All of these terms sound complicated if you are unfamiliar with them. They all involve different tax documentation and filing, as well as licensing. If you are unsure what kind of ownership you have or want, see our Accounting book.

Once you've taken the time to explain the ownership structure of your business, you should outline the profile of the owner(s). Here is the information you should include for the owner(s).

- Name
- Percentage of Ownership
- How much this person is involved in the company?
- Form of ownership (Partner, Sole Owner, Common Stock)

There will be other key people in the company who also should be part of this outline. An owner may have his or her profile expanded through this section if his or her duties include doing other things in the company.

Here is a list of the information you should collect from other employees in the company. Think of it as a resume.

- Name
- Position (description if necessary)
- Primary responsibilities in the company
- Education
- Experience and skills
- Prior employment
- Industry recognition/special skills

- Community involvement or community service
- Number of years with the company
- Compensation or salary
- Other achievements, as you deem fit

If you have a Board of Directors, you should include their resumes as well, and outline their positions on the board. You should note that the position is unpaid and the board is working in an advisory role to the business.

Organizing your business is a vital piece of the puzzle, because it requires you to take everyone that is involved in the business and assign and define each person's role. In the beginning, sometimes organizations can be a "mishmash" of people and jobs, but as you become more organized everyone finds their proper place.

| 5 |
Service/Product Line & Marketing

Next, we are going to discuss your service and product line, as well as your marketing and sales management. These are two very important pieces of your business plan.

fig. 5

Part 5 : Service & Product Line

This section describes what you are offering the consumer. Here is your chance to take an entire section of your business plan and sell your product or service. Isn't that what you've wanted to do from the beginning? Here are the things you need to include in this section:

General Description

First, give your reader a general description of your product or service. Think about it from a customer's perspective. If she has never seen your product before, what would she want to know?

Describe it to her. Talk about the current state of your product. Is it still in a prototype stage, or just an idea? What are the benefits of your product?

Lifecycle of the Product

Spend a few minutes discussing the lifecycle of your product. The product lifecycle represents the progression of a product through 4 stages. These stages are introduction, growth, maturity, and decline. During the introduction stage there is a great deal of market establishment. Pricing may be low to capture market share, or high to recover the costs of development. Promotion is aimed at new customers, investors, and advocates. Distribution (or place) is selective until consumers display a broader interest. The product itself is still in post-development stages.

During the growth period, pricing is stable and constant. Growth represents a product's acceptance by a wider range of consumers. Promotion, too, is aimed at a wider range of targets and demographics. The place portion of the marketing mix includes the addition of new channels of distribution to capture the product's market growth. The product portion of the marketing mix during the growth stage represents a period of improved quality control with the potential to add expanded services and support.

The maturity stage of the product lifecycle represents a product that has undergone some additional development in order to differentiate it from competing products. Distribution will become more competitive, and companies with mature product lines are often forced to offer incentives to control distribution over competitors. Pricing fluctuates and is often lower to maintain a competitive stance. The promotion portion of the marketing mix is heavily focused on conveying the product's level of differentiation from competitive offerings.

The decline stage of a product's lifecycle is inevitable. This does not always signal the end of a product line. Companies are faced with some options:

- Add new features or find new uses for the product to rejuvenate sales.

- Reduce costs, distribution, and promotion. Offer the product only to a loyal customer portion of the market. This is known as "harvesting" the product.

- End the product line. Discontinue production, liquidate on-hand stock, and sell the line to a company that is willing to continue production.

- The length of the product lifecycle from introduction to decline can vary drastically based on the type of product line, the industry, the target market, industry competition, and other economic factors.

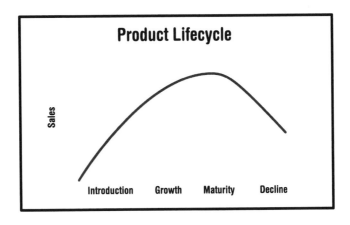

Copyright & Patent

Have you gone through the process of patenting or copyrighting your product? Do you have any pending patents? If so, you need to list them in this section. If you are planning on applying for patents, you also need to state this. If you have any legal agreements with any other parties regarding your products, you need to make that known here as well.

Research & Development

Are you working on anything else? Is there something new on the horizon in the same industry that you are planning to introduce down the road? Entice your readers with your plan. What other research and development activities can your readers anticipate from you in the future, for this business and potentially others? This is your service and product line section. It isn't very long, perhaps a page to a page and half, but it is important. It includes very valuable information to help you to sell your product and entice your reader to come on board with you.

fig. 7

Part 6 : Marketing & Sales Management

This section will probably be a little lengthy. This is where you will outline your marketing and sales strategy for your business. If sales and marketing is new to you, you'll need to do some extensive research on the topic in order to feel comfortable with tactics and ideas. You can pay outside companies or individuals to do your marketing, but that could be costly and perhaps not amenable to your budget. The price might be worth it, however, if you need assistance reaching your target market.

As you create your marketing strategy, you are creating the process that is going to get customers in the door. This is how you will turn a profit and stay in business. There is no one way to do it, but there are four keys that will help make your marketing strategy more successful.

A Penetration Strategy

You need some sort of strategy when you first open your doors. There are several, and you'll have to find and pick your favorite, but the important thing is that you do something that tells your target market that you are here and open for business.

A Growth Strategy

This is strategy that you use to help build your business. It can be anything from franchising to buying out another business. You are simply looking for opportunities to make your business grow.

Channels of Distribution Strategy

How will you get your products and services to customers? It can be through retailers, distributors, or via your own sales team.

Communication Strategy

This is the marketing strategy that you use to talk to your customers. Are you going to put a commercial on television? Ads in the newspaper? What about a billboard? You need to find ways to reach your customers and let them know you are in the neighborhood and open for business.

Now that you have your marketing strategy put together, you can go to work on your sales strategy. The sales strategy is what takes place after the customers walk through the door.

You'll need to identify a sales strategy for your sales team.

How will it work? Are you going to give the team incentives for the number of sales they make? Are they going to work on a commission basis? Are you going to give weekly or monthly bonuses for the most successful employees?

What other sales strategies are you going to use?

Think about different strategies you've experienced in your lifetime. Some employees approach you and ask if they can help you as you enter a store, others don't bother you at all. Some walk you through your entire shopping trip from beginning to end. What kind of employees do you want in your business? Look at the strategies of successful retailers or others in your industry to see which you would like to mimic.

After you have put together your sales strategies, you are ready to proceed to the next section, in which you'll assemble a funding request for your potential investors.

| 6 |
Implementation Considerations

If you are requesting funds from investors, then you will need Part 7. Otherwise, you can skip it.

Up until now, you have been working to impress potential investors, demonstrating that your business has the potential to be successful and turn a profit. Now is the time to actually make the request for the funding you need. In the section following your funding request, you will make financial projections for your business in its future years.

Part 7 : Funding Request

For many people, this is the entire reason for writing a business plan. You want to make sure to get this part right. Here is what you need to include in your funding request.

Current Funding Requirement
This is your start-up costs plus anything else you might need.

Future Funding
Outline any funding requirements that you anticipate over the next five years. Obviously, this might change, and your investors are aware of that, but be as specific as possible.

How the Money Will Be Used
Outline your funding requirements to show how the money you receive is going to be used. You've already done this with your start-

up costs, so it shouldn't be difficult to show where the money will be going. Investors want to know their money is being spent on things that are needed and truly part of the company.

Strategic Financial Plans

Outline any plans you have for the future of your company that might affect your finances. These can include a debt repayment plan, a company buyout, or selling your business. They are important, because they impact your ability to repay your loan.

Type, Term, & Time

You need to define for your investors what type of funding you would like, the time period your loan will cover, and the terms of the loan. When outlining each of these, be realistic. If you have no idea what kind of numbers to request, look online or ask your loan officer for advice. They are there to help you.

Although you won't include it in your funding request, you also will need financial information for your company. Most of this information will be placed in the next section. Mainly, you'll need to be familiar with your company's prospective financial information, which we'll complete when writing Part 8.

Part 8 : Financial Projections

You've put together a great business plan, and you're down to the final piece, your financial projections. While this piece seems simple enough, in reality, it can feel a little overwhelming.

The financial projections portion of your business plan allows you to look down the road and make an educated guess as to where your profits will be a year from now, two years from now, and so on, up to five years in the future. It isn't always easy to project. However, now that you've analyzed the market and you know more about where your business fits in the overall scheme, you have a better idea of your business' potential. Let's go through some specifics that need to be included in this section.

Historical Financial Data

This only applies if you already own an established business. If you do, you'll need to include approximately three to five years of data. You will need to include things like income statements, balance sheets, and cash flow statements. You also want to present any loan information, especially if your business had the liquidity or solvency to pay your debts on time and in full. Financial solvency is like long-term liquidity; it is the management and ability of assets to pay long-term debts (notes payable) and to sustain long-term growth.

Prospective Financial Data

Again, investors want to see what you expect your company to achieve in the foreseeable future, so create charts, graphs and text that will explain and support where you think your company will be in five years. For the first year, break it down by quarter, then annually for years two through five.

You should include mock income statements, balance sheets, cash flow statements, and capital expenditure budgets. Don't be afraid to include graphs or charts to help illustrate your points. Have a business mentor, accountant, or professional look over your proposals to proofread for errors.

Although Part 8 of your business plan can be intimidating because you are making so many assumptions, try not to feel overwhelmed. Work through it piece by piece, and this section will come together.

| 7 |

Business Plan Appendix

An appendix is not a required part of a business plan, although most people find it necessary, because there are several important pieces of research and data that don't fit or are too bulky to be placed elsewhere in the document. If you are interested in this piece and feel that it is necessary, add it to your plan. Otherwise you are welcome to skip Part 9.

Part 9 : Appendix

The appendix can include a myriad of different information relating to your overall business plan. It can be very helpful as a reference throughout your business plan, and your reader can choose to look in the appendix for further information if he or she is interested.

Your business plan is going to be seen by many different people, but not everything in your plan will apply to everyone. Some documents may apply to your investors or creditors, while other documents may only be important to potential employees. You want the documents easily referenced for appropriate readers, but you may not want everyone to have to look through all your documents.

Here are some documents that you may include in an Appendix:

- Credit reports/history (personal & business)
- Resumes
- Product pictures
- Letters of reference
- Market studies
- Licenses, permits, patents
- Copies of leases
- Building permits
- Contracts

| 8 |
Helpful Forms & Online Resources

Writing a business plan isn't easy, and it takes a lot of time and patience. There are several great online resources available, including templates and websites that others have put together to help you as you write your plan.

- *entrepreneur.com* : offers several templates to help business owners get started. You can download these into a Word document and customize them to fit your own needs.

- *bplans.com* : has sample plans that you can browse and use to help create your own business plan. They even have different categories of sample plans, which will allow you to find a business plan that will be the closest to your own. These are resources that allow you to view how owners of similar businesses have crafted their plans and put together their information and research. Bplans.com has put together a site full of business planning calculators that will help you through the planning process. It has a calculator to assist with assessing cash flow, another for start-up costs, and even a calculator for email marketing.

- *Smarta.com* : also has more than 500 sample business plans that you can reference as you are writing your own. Their plans are excellent resources, and they seem to have a business plan for just about any business imaginable. Smarta is also partnered with a business planning software company, Live Plan, with resources you can download for a fee and use to write your business plan. To see the business plans Smarta has available, click Smarta Business Plan Samples.

- *Kickstarter* : is another helpful website for those just getting started. They offer just about anything from tax estimate and 401k loan calculators to expense reports and finance statements. It's ideal for helping you keep track of things and make projections.

All in all, there are many online resources available for you. Jump online and see what you can find if you're feeling discouraged or stuck.

| 9 |
Moving Forward

Throughout this book we've talked about writing your business plan. Obviously, writing a business plan is the first step to sharing your business with investors. Once you've completed the plan and are ready to present it, you will need to put it in front of the right people. Take a look at the following recommendations.

1. Generate Leads & Referrals

Networking generates all manner of assets for businesses both new and established. Search for names, addresses and phone numbers to find the types of investors that would be interested in financing your business. Ask people you know for referrals, both for business relationships and for potential investors. Go to networking meet-ups in your chosen area.

2. Research Your Audience

Just as you researched your target market of customers, look into investors' records of spending and what industries interest them. If you are opening an apparel shop, for example, you don't want to hit an investor that only supports high-tech businesses.

3. Introduce Yourself Before Pitching.

Don't send potential investors an unsolicited business plan with a cover letter. Send an introductory email or letter to introduce yourself and allow your lead time to respond to you. Mention the opportunity with which you wish to acquaint him and let him know you have done your homework. Explain why you have selected him as a partner and why you think it will be a mutually beneficial venture should you decide to from a financial relationship.

If you're contacting him as the result of a personal referral, inform him as to who gave him the positive reference. Explain the type of business relationship you want to pursue. Are you looking for a financier, a partner, a supplier, distribution rights? Telling him up front can save both parties time if by chance your lead is a poor fit for your needs. Don't forget weekly follow-ups. If after several weeks a response isn't forthcoming, then it may be time to look elsewhere to fill your needs. Blindly sending out business plans will yield poor results. It is better to develop a relationship with quality and committed investors.

4. Meet People in Person Whenever Possible.

Meeting in person allows you to better convey your personality, energy, and passion. It also allows you to better secure commitments and leave a lasting impression.

5. Overcome Objections.

Any salesman will tell you that objections are a natural and welcome part of the persuasion process. Objections represent areas that are unclear to your audience, and this is proof positive that your audience is engaged and listening. Your job is to overcome the objections.

Of course, you have covered all of your bases and explained everything thoroughly, but questions will arise no matter how comprehensive you have been. Plan ahead by presenting your plan to friends, professionals, and mentors, and encourage them to pick apart your presentation in a devil's advocate-type setting. Simply request that they provide honest, constructive criticism that will help you when it comes time to make the real presentation.

6. *Take a Page from the Salesman's Book.*

Think of your business plan as a sales pitch. You are working toward one thing as the ultimate goal: a commitment. You won't get a commitment unless you ask for it. Encourage the commitment to be immediate. Research effective sales techniques such as the "the three yes" method of closing sales. The method is outlined below as an example.

- *"You see that I have done my due diligence right?"*

- *"You see how this business has growth potential and can be a magnet for customers?"*

- *"I'm ready to move on this opportunity, can we get this signed and started today?"*

Through asking questions that are all answered in the affirmative you bring the word "yes" to the forefront of your lead's mind and put her in an "affirmative" mindset. This is just one of hundreds of different sales persuasion tactics available to you, and taking your time to research and develop your pitch will help you consistently win over investors as well as clients and prospects.

7. *Always Operate Your Business with Impeccable Integrity.*

This is your name, your business and your reputation on the line. Word gets around fast if you're not a stand-up business partner, and a poor reputation can be disastrous for business. Consider taking a business ethics course or research business ethics and ethical business practices for more information.

Also, consider these habits of successful entrepreneurs.

1. Evaluate Your Decisions & Priorities Daily

This doesn't mean constantly question yourself, but always check to see that you're headed in the right direction. Do you have access to new information? Has the environment changed since you made your goals? What has developed that may merit leverage or require a response?

2. Always Seek New Experiences

Newness is how we learn, and we grow through learning. If your business is an extension of you, or the collaborative efforts of you and your team, your business can't learn and grow unless you learn and grow.

3. Don't Be Afraid to Leap

There will be a time when you have to take a leap of faith. It is inevitable as an entrepreneur. Don't throw yourself into everything with faith as your only research; understand the risk and reward connected to every decision so that when the time comes you can jump in with your eyes open and land on your feet.

4. Always Be on the Lookout for Opportunity

By definition, opportunity is time-sensitive. It will dissolve, expire, or the window will close. So many success stories are built on leveraging one particular opportunity that ignoring opportunities in general is downright bad for business.

5. Honestly Evaluate Your Strengths & Weaknesses.

Knowing where you excel and knowing where you need improvement is critical to personal development and is intrinsically tied to your personal and professional success. Knowing where you need improvement means that you can focus your efforts on developing your skills in a meaningful way and not dodging development that strays out of your comfort zone. Additionally, never see your progress as being at an end. When you have mastered the areas that you determined deficient, start over again to make sure that you are the very best that you can be.

conclusion

Starting your business can be as exciting as it is stressful. It takes lots of work, dedication, and research. If you keep an open mind, and you are willing to learn and grow, your dream of being your own boss and a successful entrepreneur can become a reality. If at first you fail, don't give up hope. Learn from your mistakes and remember that a mistake is truly only made once. If you do it a second time, it becomes a choice.

Remember too that once the business planning is done and you're up and running, the work isn't over. A whole new set of challenges awaits you, but with an open mind, a desire to learn, and a passion to make your dreams come true, you will succeed.

about clydebank

We are a multi-media publishing company that provides reliable, high-quality and easily accessible information to a global customer base. Developed out of the need for beginner-friendly content that is accessible across multiple formats, we deliver reliable, up-to-date, high-quality information through our multiple product offerings.

Through our strategic partnerships with some of the world's largest retailers, we are able to simplify the learning process for customers around the world, providing them with an authoritative source of information for the subjects that matter to them. Our end-user focused philosophy puts the satisfaction of our customers at the forefront of our mission. We are committed to creating multi-media products that allow our customers to learn what they want, when they want and how they want.

ClydeBank Business is a division of the multimedia-publishing firm ClydeBank Media LLC. ClydeBank Media's goal is to provide affordable, accessible information to a global market through different forms of media such as eBooks, paperback books and audio books. Company divisions are based on subject matter, each consisting of a dedicated team of researchers, writers, editors and designers.

For more information, please visit us at :
www.clydebankmedia.com
or contact *info@clydebankmedia.com*

Your world, simplified.

notes

REMEMBER TO DOWNLOAD YOUR FREE DIGITAL ASSETS!

Visit the URL below to access your free Digital Asset files that are included with the purchase of this book.

☑ Summaries   ☑ White Papers
☑ Cheat Sheets   ☑ Charts & Graphs
☑ Articles   ☑ Reference Materials

DOWNLOAD YOURS HERE:

www.clydebankmedia.com/businessplan-assets

Explore the World of
BUSINESS

TO EXPLORE ALL TITLES, VISIT:

www.clydebankmedia.com/shop

AdoptAClassroom.org

ClydeBank Media is a Proud Sponsor of

AdoptAClassroom.org

AdoptAClassroom.org empowers teachers by providing the classroom supplies and materials needed to help their students learn and succeed. As an award-winning 501(c)(3), AdoptAClassroom.org makes it easy for individual donors and corporate sponsors to donate funds to K-12 classrooms in public, private and charter schools throughout the U.S.

On average, teachers spend $600 of their own money each year to equip their classrooms – 20% of teachers spend more than $1000 annually. Since 1998 AdoptAClassroom.org has raised more than $30 million and benefited more than 4.25 million students. AdoptAClassroom.org holds a 4-star rating from Charity Navigator.

TO LEARN MORE, VISIT ADOPTACLASSROOM.ORG